DOWN IN MISSISSIPPI

BY CARLYLE BROWN

★

DRAMATISTS
PLAY SERVICE
INC.

DOWN IN MISSISSIPPI
Copyright © 2018, Carlyle Brown

All Rights Reserved

SPECIAL NOTE

SPECIAL NOTE ON SONGS AND RECORDINGS

2

DOWN IN MISSISSIPPI was developed by the Playwrights' Center and presented by Carlyle Brown & Company at the East Side Freedom Library in March 2017. It was directed by Noël Raymond, the lighting design was by Mike Wangen, the sound design was by C. Andrew Mayer, the costume design was by Clare Brauch, the prop design & installation art were by Kellie Larson, and the stage manager was April Harding. The cast was as follows:

JIMMY .... Mikell Sapp
JOHN .... Tony Sarnicki
ELLEN .... Adelin Phelps
SINGER/FANNY LOU HAMER .... Mari Harris

DOWN IN MISSISSIPPI was a commission from the Theater Department in the School of Fine Arts and the Center for American and World Cultures, Miami University of Ohio.

CHARACTERS

JIMMY

JOHN

ELLEN

DOWN IN MISSISSIPPI SONGS*

The songs in *Down in Mississippi* are very specific to the times and necessary to the plot, action, and evocation of feelings expressed throughout in the play. These songs were consciously sung to remind Civil Rights activists of their collective purpose, to give them faith, courage, and a mutual bond in the face of mortal dangers.

—Carlyle Brown

*Please see the note on songs/recordings at the back of this volume. All the songs suggested for use in *Down in Mississippi* are suggestions only; rights must be acquired from the copyright holder to use any copyrighted song in your production. Songs in the public domain may be substituted in any instance of a suggested copyrighted song.

"He who learns must suffer. And even in our sleep, pain that cannot forget falls drop by drop upon the heart, and in our despair, against our will comes wisdom to us by the awful grace of God."

—Aeschylus

DOWN IN MISSISSIPPI

A song like "Down in Mississippi" plays.

Scene 1

JIMMY. When I was a kid I used to so much admire all those white heroes in the movies and on TV who believed in something so completely that they would die for that cause. Hopalong Cassidy, Gene Autry, Roy Rogers, and the Lone Ranger and his Indian companion Tonto, heroes who were risking their lives for the cause of Freedom and Justice and the American way. …That was in the fifties and little did I know that I had something close to me like that, as close to me as the color of my skin. There was two things I seen that made me change my mind about who was and who was not a hero. The first was how they killed fourteen-year-old Emmett Till down in Leflore County down there in Mississippi. They showed him right there in *Jet* magazine, his face mangled like an old, dried-up rotten potato 'cause they said that he had whistled at a white woman. Just thinking about that just fills me up with nothing but fear and hate. …And I don't much like that feeling. That feeling like you've been cut off at the knees and you're just a suspended torso floating in the air where there is no sense of feeling for anything but fear. It's just too overwhelming. I can only fill up with so much fear and so much hate and then I got to fight. Trouble is that any Negro who is ready to fight, on any level, has a very short life span here in these United States of America. So you sit on that fear and you sit on that hate like a steaming volcano just ready to explode. …I didn't even want to think about it. I just put it right out of my head. I was just glad that I was a nigger in the Big Apple and wasn't a nigger in Mississippi. …But, then I seen something on the TV, on the news, that made me change my thinking once again. It was a little girl going to school, a little black girl going to school. It was her first day. She was six years old going to the first grade at William Frantz Elementary School in New Orleans of all places. But she wasn't just going to school, she was integrating that school, escorted by Federal Marshals no less, and every day all around her there was this mob of red-faced angry crackers yelling at her and jeering at her and threatening her life. And I'm wondering to myself how can she do it? How could she contain all that fear in that little body? How could that little girl possibly put up a wall against all that hate? How could a child so little so young have such mastery over her self? They say her momma told her to pray for them crackers 'cause what they was doing to her was the same thing they did to Jesus. I don't know about all that, but the one thing I do know from watching that little girl on the glow of that TV was that she wasn't just going to that school for herself, she was doing that for me, for all of us, for all Black people. And seeing that little girl going through all her struggles and still standing up, made me suddenly realize that she had just changed my life forever. ...So now I'm going down, down to Mississippi, down in Mississippi where a Negro is lower than a dog, his life ain't worth a nickel, and he better not complain about it. That's what I'm doing out here at Western College in Oxford, Ohio, of all places preparing and training to do that. Training with SNCC, the Student Nonviolent Coordinating Committee, Black folks, and we going down to Mississippi to register Negroes to vote no matter what them crackers say. I'm going to prove to myself that there's a light shining in me just like there was in that little girl. The only problem is that our leaders, they say we got to be nonviolent which isn't natural. Why the first law of nature is that most natural and absolute of laws, the law of self-defense. But the SNCC people say if I'm going to be with the program, I got to get with the program. They say I got to learn it, got to practice it like a discipline. Learn it like it was an instinct. 'Cause you can't fake it. It's got to be real. They say, you've got to give up that power within you and surrender it to love.

Lights up on John.

JOHN. Nigger!! Come over here! ...Boy, don't you hear me talking to you I said get your ass over here! Boy! What's your name?

8

JIMMY. Jimmy Waits sir...

JOHN. Nigger, where you from?

JIMMY. I'm from New York City sir.

JOHN. New York City? You must be lost boy. You must a took a wrong turn in the road, 'cause you a long way from New York City now. This is Mississippi and what the hell you doing here anyhow?

JIMMY. I'm here to help register Mississippi Negroes to vote in the next general election.

JOHN. Register niggers to vote? How old are you nigger?

JIMMY. I'm twenty-one years old sir.

JOHN. Twenty-one years old? Goddamn nigger twenty-one years old barely old enough to register himself, come down here to get other niggers to register to vote. Boy, if I had you over by my way I'd just go on and kill you. Niggers down here don't need to vote. And before I let you goddamned nigger communist son of a bitches come down here and start stirring things up where everything is fine, I'll just kill your black ass. You understand me boy?

JIMMY. Yes sir.

JOHN. If you want to help some niggers, why don't you help them niggers up north where you come from? ...I know what you integrationist niggers really want. It's white women, isn't it? That's what you all is doing all this for is 'cause you want our white women. Well, let me tell you boy white women is going to be the death of you yet.

JIMMY. Yes sir.

JOHN. Besides you can't have do with our white women the way I can have do with your nigger momma.

Jimmy pushes John.

JIMMY. You son of a...

JOHN. Hey Jimmy. What are you doing?

JIMMY. What am I doing? What are you doing, that's what I want to know.

JOHN. We're roleplaying here.

JIMMY. Oh yeah. Well, you're playing your role pretty damn good.

JOHN. What the hell is that suppose to mean?

9

JIMMY. You know what it means John. You're the one who's saying these words, giving them meaning and feeling. This isn't some script that somebody wrote down for you. You must know something about this.

JOHN. Look Jimmy I'm not even going to get into this with you. I didn't ask for this. I'm just following orders. Folks on the staff say you need your own personal nonviolent training. That you need special treatment, because they say you have some serious anger issues.

JIMMY. I DON'T GOT NO GODDAMN ANGER ISSUES!!!

JOHN. Their point exactly…and another thing… No cussing.

JIMMY. No cussing?

JOHN. No cussing. Profanity is against the law in Mississippi.

JIMMY. Profanity is against the law. How the hell are people going to talk?

JOHN. And it's against the law especially for you. There are lots of things in Mississippi that they can put you in jail for. We don't need our people in jail for profanity when they could be out canvassing and registering voters. Besides Mississippi Negroes are church people they don't like that kind of talk, especially calling the Lord's name in vain. They won't trust you with that kind of talk.

JIMMY. So that's why you here for the cause, is that it.

JOHN. Look Jimmy I know why I am here all right. I'm the SNCC white guy, the lowliest of the low. I'm the one that plays the stand-in for the enemy when the enemy isn't here.

JIMMY. Guilt is that it?

JOHN. Sure there's some of that. Why should I have all the privileges and opportunities just because I'm white? If you're not free then how the hell can I be?

JIMMY. …As simple as that?

JOHN. No Jimmy not simple, complicated. It's very complicated. Look, I haven't been in SNCC for very long, but I've been to jail, shot at, called a nigger lover. Whatever you think of me I'm here. This isn't about me or you even, this is about the movement. If you can't get with the program you've got to go.

JIMMY. I've got to go!

JOHN. ...Look Jimmy those Mississippi Southerners will smell a guy like you a mile away. Your pride, your sense of dignity, your self-assuredness, they'll kill you for that Jimmy. They can't spread their fear with guys like you walking around. They'll kill you. ...And then we'll have to bury you and have a funeral where we will laud about what a great hero you were for the cause and then we'll have to go back out in the rural communities to try to quiet people's fears and have to start all over again.

JIMMY. I don't get this. You're telling me how violent and vicious these people are and you're saying I've got to be completely passive.

JOHN. It isn't passive it's resistance, passive resistance. It isn't like we're not doing anything. It's action, we're taking action and bit by bit we're making change.

JIMMY. What are you some kind of pacifist?

JOHN. Yeah, I'm a pacifist my family are Quakers.

JIMMY. ...Quakers?

JOHN. Yeah Quakers, I mean what good does killing do?

JIMMY. It means that there's one less of them to brutalize you.

JOHN. And then there're ten more of them to take their place and that only means more black bodies laying dead in the Delta swamps or drowned in a river. Nonviolence is the only way. It's the SNCC way. And it's the only way if you're going to be part of SNCC.

JIMMY. ...The only way?

JOHN. Yes, the only way.

JIMMY. So, what do I have to do?

JOHN. Take the abuse.

JIMMY. And how do I do that?

JOHN. I don't know. That's up to you. It's your choice.

JIMMY. Well you said you've been in SNCC awhile, been jailed, shot at. How do you do it?

JOHN. It's different every time.

JIMMY. So the fear and the anger they never go away?

JOHN. No they never go away.

JIMMY. Well, how does that work?

JOHN. I stand here and you stand there…

JIMMY. No, I mean how does that work in your head?

JOHN. I can't help you there Jimmy. It's different for everybody. It's personal. …Some see it as tactical.

JIMMY. …Tactical?

JOHN. Yeah, it's the only way that Negroes in Mississippi can resist.

JIMMY. You mean fight back?

JOHN. Yeah.

JIMMY. And what's that in your hand?

JOHN. It's a rubber billy club.

JIMMY. …A rubber billy club?

JOHN. Yeah.

JIMMY. Oh yeah, and what are you planning to do with that rubber billy club?

JOHN. I'm going to hit you with it.

JIMMY. Say what?

JOHN. It won't hurt it's only rubber, soft rubber. It's for the idea. It might sting a little bit but you're not afraid of a little sting are you Jimmy?

JIMMY. The hell with you John!

JOHN. No cussing.

JIMMY. Then later for you John! Let's do this.

JOHN. Nigger, are you eye-balling me? Don't be eye-balling me nigger keep your eyes down on the ground do you hear me?

JIMMY. No sir.

JOHN. Submit nigger do you hear me.

JIMMY. No sir.

JOHN. Submit I say.

JIMMY. No sir.

JOHN. Submit.

JIMMY. No sir.

A song like "We Shall Not Be Moved" plays.

Scene 2

ELLEN. You know going away to school, going away to college is a pretty scary thing. All your life you've been encouraged and spoiled and told that you're special and then all of a sudden just right out of nowhere you have to decide what you're going to do for rest of your life. It's terrible. It's terrifying. I think that that's why kids in college drink so much all the time because they're scared. I mean that's what college really teaches us more than just books and studies is that nothing is ever going to be the same like it used to be anymore. It wasn't until now that I in some way realize how much my mom had made so many sacrifices so that me and my little brother would feel that way...special I mean. But I didn't know then and I don't know now what I'm going to do with the rest of my life. I mean I'm a poli-sci major, but that's just because I read the newspapers all the time to keep from listening to my little brother whining and my mom complaining about what she has to go through. ...And now I have to do something with my life. So, I'm going down to Mississippi. I'm going to teach. I'm going to be a teacher in a Freedom School. I'm going to teach civil rights and politics and civics and Negro history and a lot of things that I don't really know anything about. But I'm learning and then I'm going to be teaching. I know my mom has still got to support me, but for now, for this summer anyway, I'm going to Mississippi. You see when I started discovering what was going on in Mississippi it really disturbed me. It hurt me in my heart. It just upset me and I couldn't stop thinking about it. It's wrong it's just wrong what those white people do to Negroes in Mississippi.
    Enter Jimmy.
JIMMY. Hello.
ELLEN. Oh hi. ...You frightened me.
JIMMY. I'm sorry.
ELLEN. No worries. I was distracted and day-dreaming anyway. I need to wake up. Ellen Bormann, Vassar class of '67.

13

JIMMY. Jimmy Waits, City College class of somewhere out there in time.

ELLEN. Yeah me too… I don't know where I'll be somewhere out there in time either. Are you here for the Mississippi Summer project?

JIMMY. Yeah.

ELLEN. Are you SNCC or a volunteer?

JIMMY. Well, I'm sort of on probation with SNCC. A kind of political purgatory you might say. So I guess I'd have to say I'm a volunteer.

ELLEN. So, you're just a volunteer?

JIMMY. You mean not a seasoned veteran of the movement?

ELLEN. Yeah, I guess so.

JIMMY. No I'm just a volunteer like you.

ELLEN. Oh…

JIMMY. Oh?

ELLEN. I'm sorry. I thought because you're a Negro that you were SNCC. I don't know why I thought that. I mean not all Negroes are SNCC and you're a Negro and you're a volunteer just like me. It was silly. I'm sorry.

JIMMY. No worries Miss Ellen.

ELLEN. Please, don't do that?

JIMMY. Don't do what?

ELLEN. Don't do that. Don't call me "Miss Ellen." I know what that means. Like "Miss Ann" or Master or Boss and stuff like that. Yeah, my mom has a maid and she's Negro. Her name is Sara and we pay her fair and treat her with respect. So, I won't call you "boy" if you don't call me "Miss Ellen."

JIMMY. All right "Miss Ellen" all right. But I bet you Sara calls you Miss Ellen.

ELLEN. Stop it.

JIMMY. All right Ellen all right. I'm sorry.

ELLEN. …No, I'm sorry.

JIMMY. You're sorry? Sorry for what?

14

ELLEN. I don't know. I'm just sorry that's all. I shouldn't have gone on like that.

JIMMY. It's all right Ellen. We're all a little skittish at the moment. We all don't know what's coming down the road for us. Don't know what's going to happen to us.

ELLEN. I know that's right. That's what Sara always says, "I know that's right."

JIMMY. ...Sara the maid?

ELLEN. ...Yeah, Sara our maid.

JIMMY. She sounds like she's a wise woman.

ELLEN. She is a wise woman. She quotes this poem by Aeschylus every now and again. I don't know where she learned it, but she's got it memorized and she says it now and again. She folds her hands in front of her, holds her head up and like a prophet she says it. ..."He who learns must suffer. And even in our sleep, pain that cannot forget falls drop by drop upon the heart, and in our despair, against our will comes wisdom to us by the awful grace of God."

JIMMY. Wow.

ELLEN. Yeah.

JIMMY. So you go to Vassar, your mom has a maid...and where are you from?

ELLEN. I'm from Boston. My mom and my dad just got divorced a few years ago. He's a lawyer. He's the one that makes all the money. I'm a political science major. I think I want to teach. I don't know.

JIMMY. Tell me something.

ELLEN. What?

JIMMY. What are you doing here?

ELLEN. You want to know the truth?

JIMMY. Yeah, I do.

ELLEN. I don't really know why I'm here. I guess I'm here to find that out.

JIMMY. You know it could be dangerous?

ELLEN. Yeah.

JIMMY. Like get yourself beaten, brutalized, and killed dangerous.

ELLEN. Yes, I know that.

JIMMY. And you're here just the same?

ELLEN. For now anyway...

JIMMY. Pleased to meet you Miss Ellen Bormann.

ELLEN. Pleased to meet you Mr. Jimmy... Mr. Jimmy Waits I mean.

Enter John.

JOHN. Oh, hey... Hello.

JIMMY. Oh John. John this Ellen, Vassar, class of '67.

ELLEN. ...Which is yet to be.

JIMMY. ...Which is yet to be. Ellen this is John...John is SNCC.

ELLEN. John is SNCC?

JIMMY. John is SNCC.

Jimmy and Ellen laugh.

JOHN. I don't get it.

ELLEN. It's just a little joke we were having about how nothing is ever what you expect it to be. Pleased to meet you John?

JOHN. Alexander. John Alexander is my name. I...I went to Oberlin. I graduated. And ah you too...I mean me too...I mean I'm pleased to meet you too. ...Listen, have you guys heard about the three missing workers?

ELLEN. Missing workers?

JIMMY. Yeah, I heard three guys drove down to Meridian this weekend. To investigate a church burning or something like that.

ELLEN. Someone burned a church?

JIMMY. And these guys are missing?

JOHN. I didn't want to say "missing." It's just that we haven't heard from them and we're concerned. We thought everybody should know. There's going to be a meeting...

ELLEN. You're saying you're concerned. Concerned about what? Do you think something has happened to them?

JOHN. We're a little concerned. It's Mississippi.

ELLEN. Oh my God.

JIMMY. What are we going to do about it?

16

JOHN. What are we going to do about it? We're just going to keep doing what we set out to do, register Negroes in Mississippi to vote. That's what we're going to do. That's what the meeting is for, to say that I guess. And to let people know that we understand if they don't want to go.

ELLEN. And we have to choose now.

JOHN. We have to choose now. ...Well Jimmy, are you going?

JIMMY. John, don't even ask me that okay. But since you feel the need to be so direct about it, about asking it of me, I'll explain it to you okay. I have no intention of walking down that road and living the life that would happen to me if I turn away from here now. That's one death that I don't want to deal with. I'd rather deal with some other kind of death, 'cause we all got to deal with that...death. In this life nobody gets out alive. I'm already past that point you talking about. I'm dealing with something else altogether now. So, you don't need to prop yourself up getting yourself ready to preach at me.

JOHN. I'm not preaching at you Jimmy, I'm only asking. You just told me and now I know.

JIMMY. And now you know? You don't know. You'll never know.

ELLEN. Hey guys. Guys, come on guys. We're all in this together.

JIMMY. I knew Ellen would still go.

JOHN. How do you know that?

JIMMY. We've been having a little chat and I know. Isn't that right Ellen?

ELLEN. Well, I'm not so sure that I do. I mean I've never known violence. I can't even stand to watch a fist-fight on the television. Boxing, football, hockey, they all make me sick. It's just brutal and desperate and ugly. I'm just not sure. I don't know what I'm going to do. And we have to decide now? ...Look John, Jimmy, I'm puking all over myself here. You're going to just have to excuse me. I need to be alone for a while.

Exit Ellen.

JOHN. Jimmy, are you hitting on that girl?

JIMMY. Say what?

JOHN. Are you hitting on her? You know what I'm talking about.

17

JIMMY. Well, my question to you is what if I were and what the hell is it to you?

JOHN. No, no, I'm not trying to get into your business. But if there is one thing, maybe the only thing, the prime directive of the movement is no interracial relationships. No miscegenation, no holding hands, no walking together, no being together…no sex, no relations of any kind. In Mississippi that would be a disaster.

JIMMY. You must think I live in some kind of hole somewhere not to know that. I knew that before the first time you ever laid eyes on somebody's Negro. What makes you think I want anything to do with your skanky-ass white girl?

JOHN. Now come on you don't have to call her that.

JIMMY. Maybe you've got a thing for her yourself?

JOHN. Me? …For her? …No.

JIMMY. Maybe that's the problem you have with me hitting on her as you say.

JOHN. I've never seen her before. We just met. You introduced us.

JIMMY. …Like the problem you've got with authority.

JOHN. …Authority?

JIMMY. Yeah, that you don't have any…that you're working for Black folks, Negroes as you call us and when something gets decided you don't get to decide it. That's what's bothering you. It's bugging you so much that you have to take your authority Jones out on me.

JOHN. That's crazy. I don't feel that way.

JIMMY. Come on John this is America everybody feels that way.

JOHN. Oh Jimmy I'm telling you it's really hard to be a pacifist around you. What are you so angry at?

JIMMY. Guess?

JOHN. I can't do anything about that. I don't understand it. I can't even imagine it. It just won't fit in my head. I don't know what to say. I'm sorry. But I'm here and I'm trying, so what do you want from me?

JIMMY. You know it's so easy for you guys. You can say it, say it and mean it, mean it deep in your heart but at the end of the day you can always choose to say it and not mean it or not say it at all. We don't get to do that.

JOHN. I know.

JIMMY. There you go again. You know. What you think you know like James Baldwin says is that you think you know my experience better than I do. Look, I've never been to Mississippi John, but I live in America and Mississippi seems to me just a place in America where they keep their hate real. And you seem to feel that you can instruct me on this based on your subjective experience as a white man. Well, I'm telling you John I can see where I'm starting to get the hang of this nonviolence thing 'cause it's the only thing keeping me from kicking a hole in you. Do you understand me John? …A big black hole.

Enter Ellen.

ELLEN. John. Jimmy. We just got news about those three boys that drove down to Meridian. They found their car, a blue Ford station wagon. It was burnt and abandoned and the boys weren't in it, two white one Negro.

JIMMY. I'm sorry John.

JOHN. It's okay Jimmy, it's okay.

ELLEN. I'm going. I'm going.

Blackout.

A song like "In the Mississippi River" plays.

Scene 3

A Mississippi Freedom Summer field office. John holds a book in his hands.

JOHN. On the bus on the way down to Mississippi I finished this book I was reading, *The Rebel* by Albert Camus. It's a series of essays about the history of revolution. It says that the moment when the slave confronts his master or the oppressed confronts his oppressor is the moment when he suddenly realizes that he is not just one, but many. That in acting alone he is not alone. That it is then when he finally realizes his humanity and his humanness. And that is why in that moment of rebellion he is willing to sacrifice and suffer and face the fate of his own death to put a stop to the suffering of others, like himself. ...But that's not exactly my situation is it? For me my oppressor is invisible. He's selfish, indifferent, afraid...he's a coward, a slave to his own self-preservation. So, I guess that's why I rode on a bus to Mississippi in the dark of night reading a book about revolution on my way to meet my own oppressor. Looking for some hope in this world I guess. ...And yet, it also says in this book that the moment of rebellion, that moment most pure and absolute, a moment most noble, is only a moment. For in the sweep of time and history no sooner than the rebel rises, that that moment can become an era and an age of rage, terrorism, and revenge. I mean that's what we're all afraid of when we think of revolution and change isn't it? That the oppressed will become the oppressor and there will be suffering upon suffering on top of suffering that never stops on into the end of time, hopeless. So, I guess what this book is telling me is that it's all hopeless. If you're lucky enough to have a good life, it's hard to understand hopelessness. When you've got freedom and opportunity and a chance for success and happiness, hopelessness is hard to look at. It makes you want to look away. It's a state worse than death. It is death, a living death. And like yawning or catching a cold it can be so contagious. You would think Blacks in Mississippi would have it, but they don't. You would think that after hundreds of years of oppression that hopelessness wouldn't be just a low point in their lives, it would be all of their lives, but it isn't. Despite being beaten, brutalized, abused, murdered even, they go in groups to the courthouse to register in order to vote for a better life. And man, going down to that courthouse must be a scary thing to do. Imagine facing down a law that ruled over you and only you and applied to no other, not even to those who would reign lawless over you? If there were a system that would shape you in a world without dignity, without a sense of possibility, without joy, without hope...what would you do? Would you go down to the very courthouse where they execute those laws and say no you can't do that to me no more? Well, that's exactly what these Mississippi Black folks are doing. And how do they do that? ...I don't know, but somehow they do.

ELLEN. John...

JOHN. Oh, Ellen.

ELLEN. John, what am I suppose to do with these phone calls.

JOHN. ...Phone calls?

ELLEN. Yeah, phone calls. I'm on duty today and tonight too. I'm supposed to man the phones to take calls from volunteers reporting in from canvassing out there wherever they are. But most of the calls that come in there's no answer, there's just somebody breathing into the telephone or else screaming some horrible rant... I can't even repeat the awful things they say.

JOHN. I know. I know.

ELLEN. And here we are way out in the middle of nowhere in this old house alone on some country road.

JOHN. It's intimidation.

ELLEN. Well, it's working. And one of the callers even called me by my name. "Hello Ellen, are you safe where you are?"

JOHN. I know.

ELLEN. Can't we do something about it?

JOHN. I don't think I know what that would be.

ELLEN. Well then call the FBI. We have numbers for the local FBI. We should call them.

JOHN. The FBI won't help us. They only come when something's already happened. And when they do come and we report to them who did whatever it was they did to us, they report it to the local authorities who put it in the local newspaper, so that the Klan and the local thugs can have our names and addresses.

ELLEN. You're kidding me.

JOHN. No, I'm not.

ELLEN. Well, isn't there somebody we can call?

JOHN. The Justice Department, but I think in the great scope of things that's probably only one phone call.

ELLEN. So, nothing happens unless something happens to one of us.

JOHN. Yes, to *one of us*.

ELLEN. What do you mean by *one of us*?

JOHN. I mean to one of us, you and me, the white people on the project. Nothing is going to happen and nobody is going to do anything until something happens to one of us.

ELLEN. What?

JOHN. Negroes down here have been dying on these country roads longer than anybody can ever remember and nothing has ever been done about it. They only way it will ever get noticed...

ELLEN. ...Is if something happens to one of us?

JOHN. Yes.

ELLEN. Like some sacrificial lamb or something. ...Like those three missing workers.

JOHN. Yeah, you could say that.

ELLEN. Oh, my God.

JOHN. I wish I could tell you that everything is going to be okay.

ELLEN. Why would you want to tell me that?

JOHN. I don't know. I just do that's all.

ELLEN. You have to tell the truth otherwise we don't know how to prepare ourselves.

JOHN. Yes, that's true.

ELLEN. How do we prepare ourselves John?

JOHN. I don't know. I guess you look ahead. Look to the future. See what's in front of you. Understand what's at stake. I mean it's so hard what we're trying to do that you and I, what happens to us barely matters. You see if all the Negroes in Mississippi which there are many more of than whites, if all those Negroes had the right to vote and voted for their own interests, then everything in Mississippi would change. The neighborhoods, the schools, what is taught in the schools, the laws and the government everything will be different.

ELLEN. ...Everything?

JOHN. ...Everything.

ELLEN. And what is that going to be like?

JOHN. Nobody knows. That's why everybody's scared. Those guys on the phone they're just scared. They don't know what's going to happen if everything changes.

ELLEN. We're like trying to change the world.

JOHN. Yeah, I guess you could say that it was something like that.

ELLEN. I thought it was about voting. But that's what voting is, isn't it?

JOHN. It's supposed to be.

ELLEN. ...It's strange.

JOHN. What is?

ELLEN. It's strange how it feels so important to me, important enough for me to not feel like getting on a bus and getting as far away from here as I could. I don't know. I mean I feel like if it could happen here, it could happen anywhere.

JOHN. And it's important not just for us.

ELLEN. Yes...yeah...not just for us.

JOHN. Are you okay Ellen?

ELLEN. Oh, I'm all right. Thanks John for being so understanding. You're a smart, compassionate, and very kind person.

JOHN. Oh, I don't know. I can go on and on about that kind of stuff. I was raised that way. A family of lefties and Quakers with me stuck in the middle. I didn't have much choice.

ELLEN. You do have a choice. And you've made it and I admire you for that John.

JOHN. You do?

ELLEN. Yes, very much.

JOHN. Well, thanks. I think you're pretty brave yourself.

ELLEN. Me? No I'm not brave. I'm only here because I didn't have a clue that's all, and I'm glad I didn't. I'm glad I'm not somewhere where I did have a clue and couldn't do anything. That's where I lived. That's where I come from, a place where people don't have a clue and when they do have one, they don't do anything. I'm glad I'm not there.

JOHN. You know I like you Ellen.

ELLEN. I like you too John.

JOHN. I mean to say that I like you very much.

ELLEN. I like you too John.

Enter Jimmy.

JIMMY. Whoa! Welcome home the conquering hero!

ELLEN. ...The conquering hero?

JIMMY. Yes, the conquering hero. I got me ten for the courthouse in the morning.

JOHN. You got "ten for the courthouse in the morning"? What are you talking about Jimmy?

JIMMY. I'm talking about that we've been out there me and the SNCC people and some local people and all, been out there since early this morning. Out there walking, walking down these dusty country roads knocking on doors, going into stores, playing with their kids, we even picked us a little cotton.

ELLEN. Picking cotton where?

JIMMY. Down on that plantation down the road a ways. Man, that cotton picking that's some hard-ass work.

JOHN. No Jimmy, don't tell me you went there. That's trespassing.

JIMMY. Trespassing, transgressing our natural butts off. We're here to break the law to change the law, that's all we was doing. Man I had those colored folks laughing so hard they could barely stand up. I told them that up in New York City if we see a white boy wearing a sheet we just set it on fire. I did my imitation of that fat old courthouse clerk. "Now, you niggers don't need to be listening to those Northern agitators they ain't nothing but a bunch of communists. You all know we take care of our niggers." I told them that if that hunky, redneck, peckerwood cracker was to live in their world he wouldn't get through the day, not one day. He wouldn't last into the afternoon. I mean you can see in their hands, in their muscles, in their bones. They're some strong, hard working Black people. I mean, nobody work that hard suppose to be poor like that. I asked them what kind of food the white folks eat...soul food. What kind of talk they talk? ...Black talk, that's what they talk only with a twang. They're all up there nodding their heads and mumbling as if to say this colored boy is crazy, but I could see they know I was right. I could see the revolution in their eyes, bright, twinkling and ready for Freddy. We must have talked to fifty, sixty people and me, myself I got me ten, ten stouthearted men. Well, most of them are women, but I got me ten ready to register. I'm telling you John, Ellen I found out that I can do this thing. And now we're going to the courthouse in the morning.

A song like "We Are Soldiers" plays.

Scene 4

Later that night in the field office.

Ellen sits on a bare mattress with a flashlight in her hand. She is consumed with fear. The headlights of cars flash by windowpanes, accompanied by the sounds of their engines running, along with rebel yells and jeers from outside. There is the occasional "thud" of objects being thrown against the outside walls and perhaps once or twice the sound of breaking glass smashing through the "gobo" windowpanes. Ellen tries to master her fear, taking deep breaths, and squelching her tears, finally she begins to softly sing a song like "We Shall Overcome."

Enter Jimmy.

Ellen screams.

JIMMY. It's all right. It's okay. It's me Jimmy.

ELLEN. Jimmy! What are you doing here?

JIMMY. I came to see who was in here.

ELLEN. But, you can't stay here. If they find you here they'll kill us. They'll kill you. You've got to get out of here.

JIMMY. I don't think they saw me sneaking in here, but if I leave now it'll amount to the same thing.

ELLEN. Oh, my God. I shouldn't have stayed here alone. I shouldn't have stayed. I told everyone that I'd be all right. That I'd be right along, then I fell asleep.

JIMMY. It's okay. Get ahold of yourself. You're all right.

ELLEN. Oh, Jimmy, I'm so scared.

JIMMY. I know, I know, me too.

ELLEN. What are we going to do?

JIMMY. Just sit here, be quiet and lay low until they're gone. They'll get tired after a while. Here, let me put my arms around you.

ELLEN. But what if they see us?

JIMMY. They can't see us from outside.

ELLEN. But what if they come in here and find us?

JIMMY. We'll have to cross that bridge when it comes.

Ellen falls into Jimmy's arms.

ELLEN. Why did you come?

JIMMY. I saw them circling around so I knew somebody was in here. Then I saw your flashlight shining so I figured somebody was in here alone. I know I wouldn't want to be alone like this. Would you?

ELLEN. No.

JIMMY. It's weird huh?

ELLEN. What is?

JIMMY. It's like in the cowboy movies. Two pioneers, a man and a woman out alone on the frontier in a deserted cabin with wild Indians circling the place, with me shooting and you reloading… only now it's a black man and a white woman with wild white folks circling the place.

ELLEN. Only we're not shooting and reloading.

JIMMY. No, but I can see like in the cowboy movies we'd be picking them off pretty good.

ELLEN. What happens if they shoot flaming arrows and set the place on fire?

JIMMY. We'd go through the trap door into the cellar. There's always a trap door.

ELLEN. And what if we run out of ammunition? You'll have to save the last bullet to keep me from suffering.

JIMMY. I'd never do that. I'd fight to the last. Besides the cavalry always comes before that happens.

ELLEN. ...Always?

JIMMY. ...Always.

ELLEN. The cavalry isn't coming.

JIMMY. No.

ELLEN. The cavalry is already here. You're the cavalry Jimmy. ... You know Jimmy, I know that I'm just supposed to teach in the Freedom School and man the front office tomorrow but I want to go with all of you to the courthouse in the morning.

JIMMY. You do?

ELLEN. Yes, I do. I really do.

JIMMY. Aren't you scared?

ELLEN. Yeah, but I'll feel safe with you. Besides if I get scared, I'll sing.

A song like "We Shall Overcome" plays.

Scene 5

It is night again, in the front seat of a car. Jimmy is driving, Ellen is in the middle, and John rides shotgun.

JOHN. Jimmy what the hell is wrong with you?

ELLEN. The bastard, the miserable bastard...

JOHN. I don't believe you raised your fist to that guy.

JIMMY. I didn't hit him did I?

ELLEN. He doesn't know me. Who the hell is he to talk to me like that?

JOHN. You didn't have to hit him, raising your fists amounts to the same thing.

27

ELLEN. "What are you doing down here white girl," he says.

JIMMY. If I had hit him I would have killed him. He would have been dead. Be thankful for that.

ELLEN. "Which one of them coons you screwing."

JOHN. No, you would have been dead. We all would have been dead. You and your going to the courthouse in the morning. Only four of your stout-hearted ten showed up.

ELLEN. "Which one of those niggers are you screwing slut," he says.

JIMMY. Four is better than none.

JOHN. Yeah, and you lose control and we get arrested. The only reason they let us out of that jail was so that we could be out here on the road alone.

ELLEN. He spit in my face. That redneck bastard spit in my face.

JIMMY. Easy Ellen, take it easy.

ELLEN. Nobody's ever spoken to me like that in my life. Nobody speaks to me like that.

JOHN. Ellen you're getting hysterical. You've got to calm yourself down.

ELLEN. Fuck you John. Fuck you Mister Know-it-all. Just shut the hell up. We can see what's going on. We don't need a lecture from you, not now, not tonight.

JOHN. Ellen…

ELLEN. Jimmy was trying to defend me, to protect me. It's about feelings John. You got a problem about feelings John?

JOHN. …Feelings?

JIMMY. Whoa, everybody chill.

JOHN. You're talking about chill. I'll tell you about chill. You're the one that got us into this mess Jimmy.

JIMMY. No I'm talking about chill. There're headlights in the rear-view mirror.

JOHN. What?

JIMMY. We're being followed.

ELLEN. Oh shit. Oh shit.

JOHN. Damn and we're all sitting in the front seat together.

JIMMY. And what do you think Mister Know-it-all that we'll all be safer, that it would make a difference if you two were in the back seat and I was playing the chauffer.

JOHN. All right listen when we stop let me do all the talking. Ellen and me we'll crawl into the back seat.

JIMMY. There ain't going to be no crawling anywhere, because we ain't stopping.

ELLEN. Oh shit. Oh shit.

JOHN. Jimmy what are you doing?

JIMMY. I'm doing eighty, now eighty-five, ninety...ninety-five...a hundred.

ELLEN. Oh shit. Oh shit.

JOHN. Jimmy, are you all right?

JIMMY. I'm cool.

JOHN. Hold on man.

JIMMY. I got it.

A song like "Keep Your Eyes on the Prize" plays.

Scene 6

VOICE OF LYNDON B. JOHNSON. We believe that all men are created equal. Yet many are denied equal treatment.
We believe that all men have certain unalienable rights. Yet many Americans do not enjoy those rights.
We believe that all men are entitled to the blessings of liberty. Yet millions are being deprived of those blessing—not because of their own failures, but because of the color of their skins.

Cross fade.

Circa 1964 portable radio. John and Ellen listen.

The reasons are deeply imbedded in history and tradition and the nature of man. We can understand—without rancor or hatred—

how this all happened.

But it cannot continue. Our Constitution, the foundation of our republic, forbids it. The principles of our freedom forbid it. Morality forbids it. And the law I will sign tonight forbids it.

John turns off the radio.

ELLEN. John what are you doing?

JOHN. Politicians all they do is talk, talk, talk. Read what it says in the papers.

ELLEN. "July 2nd, 1964. Tonight President Lyndon Baines Johnson will sign a new Civil Rights bill into law. The most sweeping civil rights legislation since Reconstruction, the Civil Rights Act prohibits discrimination of all kinds based on race, color, religion, or national origin. Major features of the bill are: the barring of unequal voter registration requirements"… It's about time… "the outlawing of discrimination in hotels, motels, restaurants, theaters, and all other public accommodations engaged in interstate commerce." Oh, that's nice of them. And how are they going to do that? "Encourages desegregation of public schools"… Encourages? …Encourages. "Outlaws discrimination in employment in any business exceeding twenty-five people and creates an Equal Employment Opportunities Commission to review complaints." Oh, great. Now they'll fire everybody, kick the people off the land and make twenty-five do the work of fifty or sixty. This bill is no good. It's a worthless piece of paper. It's full of holes. It's a piece of trash.

JOHN. No, no there're a lot of good things in this bill. It's a start. It's a chance.

ELLEN. There's no enforcement. They can't enforce it. It hasn't got any teeth. We need protection. These people down here need protection and we need it now.

JOHN. Under the Constitution the states have their rights.

ELLEN. …Rights? They have no rights. They have no right to treat people the way they do down here. They have no right at all.

JOHN. You're starting to sound like Jimmy.

ELLEN. And what's wrong with that. Maybe I should sound like Jimmy every once in a while. Maybe you should sound like Jimmy every once in a while yourself.

JOHN. Ellen what's the matter?

ELLEN. Oh, nothing. I'm sorry. I just had a bad day that's all.

JOHN. Do you want to tell me about it?

ELLEN. No! No.

JOHN. Come on. Tell me about it. What happened?

ELLEN. Some of us white girls on the project went over to the local college today to talk to the white students about what we were doing here. One of the professors invited us.

JOHN. Yeah?

ELLEN. They asked a lot of questions.

JOHN. What kind of questions?

ELLEN. They asked a lot of personal questions.

JOHN. What kind of personal questions?

ELLEN. Personal questions John, personal questions.

JOHN. Okay. Okay. I'm sorry.

ELLEN. No, I'm sorry. I shouldn't have yelled at you like that. I'm not mad at you.

JOHN. Are you okay?

ELLEN. No.

JOHN. Is there anything I can do?

ELLEN. No.

Enter Jimmy.

Jimmy where have you been?

JOHN. Jimmy what's the matter?

JIMMY. Nothing's the matter. It's just another day like every other day down here, a day of fear, anger, hopelessness, just another day in the Delta.

JOHN. I know we've been working hard Jimmy, but have you heard about the Civil Rights bill? It was on broadcast tonight.

Jimmy sits down in a chair.

JIMMY. Yeah, I heard about that Civil Rights bill. That's all every-body's talking about Black and White. And do you know what signing that bill means? It means that these crackers down here are going to

31

resist. They're going to resist the law and that means there's going to be more violence and brutality and these colored folks down here are going to suffer more than they ever did before. We already supposed to have the rights what they put in that bill. And now look at us. Look what's happening to us. We're like Indians in a cowboy movie.

ELLEN. Oh, Jimmy, my poor Jimmy.

JOHN. It gets to you Jimmy. That's what happens, you see so much suffering and after a while you can't look at it anymore, you just lose it. You just can't see it anymore.

JIMMY. I just can't wrap my head around it. Why can't people just live? Why must people be persecuted just because they're Black or they're poor, never mind Black and poor? Why? I hate these white people, I swear I do. I hate 'em, I hate 'em, I hate 'em.

ELLEN. John, would you leave Jimmy and me alone for a while?

JOHN. ...Alone, but why?

ELLEN. Please John, just go.

JOHN. All right, I'll go and leave the two of you alone for a while.

John exits.

ELLEN. Jimmy it's all right. It's all right. ...Jimmy look at me. Look it at me. I have something that I have to tell you. I did something today that I am very ashamed of.

JIMMY. ...Something that you're ashamed of?

ELLEN. I lied.

JIMMY. Lied? Lied about what?

ELLEN. Some of us white girls on the project went over to the local college today to talk to the white students about what we were doing here. One of the professors invited us. They had a lot of questions... personal questions. Questions about how we felt about what we were doing down here. Questions about how we felt about Negroes. One of the girls asked me could I be friendly with one, would I marry one. Could I actually love a Negro? And what I'm ashamed of is that I lied and told her no.

JIMMY. Lied? But, lied about what?

ELLEN. Lied about whether I could actually love a Negro, because the truth is that I love you Jimmy.

JIMMY. ...Ellen.

ELLEN. It's all right Jimmy. You don't have to give it back to me. It's already in me. It's already mine. I love you and when that racist Southern white girl in that class asked me that question I realized that I knew the answer from that first day I met you in that hallway at Western College when you were testing me, testing that little white girl Miss Ellen.

JIMMY. Ellen, I...I don't know what to say.

ELLEN. Please Jimmy, just feel safe about it feel safe with it. I know that it's a dangerous and foolish thing this thing between the two of us. But I love you Jimmy. And you don't owe me anything for it. It isn't mysterious really, even though it is mysterious. It's love. It just is.

JIMMY. Yeah. It just is.

Scene 7

JOHN. They say that freedom is a constant struggle. They say that love is a constant struggle... Love? What is it? What is it that makes you feel that you can look deep within your soul? Is it the pain? Is it the loneliness? What is it? What makes us think we can know ourselves, our true identities or that of our neighbor or someone we love? What is it? I have to be, I am forced to be who I am and a white guy is who I am. It isn't my fault, I didn't ask for this any more than anybody else. It's the card I was dealt, I'm a white guy. And I know a good deal of suffering in the world is caused by white guys. I get that. But I'm not that white guy. I don't know what it is about Ellen. I don't know what it is. I get this feeling for her. I can't express it. But when I think about her and Jimmy together it all goes wrong inside of me. I get this feeling in me that no matter how hard I try I just can't get rid of it. I know it's because it's been embedded in me from all these years of history and politics in this country and I know that feeling in me isn't really me it's the other white guy. Yeah, it's him the other guy, the one in the mirror. That's the last thing I ever wanted to be was that guy. And now here he is looking me in the face. When I go out here and talk to the rural Black folk around

33

here they're always bowing their heads, scraping their feet and calling me "sir" and "boss." I want to say no that's not me it's the other white guy. And the Black folk on the project are always questioning my motives. Why, because I'm a white guy. Even though I get threatened, beat up, and thrown in jail just like everybody else. It starts to seem like a white guy can't do anything right. And when I complain about it do you know what they tell me? "Now you know how it feels." Seems like a hurtful thing to say. But it's true and it's painful. And no matter what I do I'm going to do everything I can not to be that other white guy. Because you see, you can be so wrong about people. All I wanted was Jimmy's respect and instead he gave me his love.

John puts on a light summer jacket he has been holding and when he has put it on we see that it is covered in blood.

Lights up. Jimmy and Ellen in the back seat of a car.

ELLEN. John! John, get in! Hurry!

John gets in the car behind the wheel.

Driving.

JOHN. The bastards, those filthy bastards won't admit him in the hospital. No coloreds he says.

ELLEN. Do you know of another one?

JOHN. Yes, I know. We're going there now.

ELLEN. Is it far?

JOHN. It's a ways. Not too far.

ELLEN. Don't go too fast John. Don't speed. We don't want them to stop us.

JOHN. I'm doing the best I can Ellen.

ELLEN. I know, I know.

JOHN. Why did you do it Jimmy? Why did you throw your body on top of me like that?

JIMMY. Those people were trying to hurt you John. We're supposed to protect each other.

JOHN. Yeah, but they beat the crap out of you man. They wouldn't have beaten me that bad. They wouldn't have beaten me like that.

JIMMY. Well I wasn't going to sit back and find out.

JOHN. Those bastards, those cracker bastards, those redneck peckerwood bastards, I wish I could kill every one of them, everyone. Kill them all and give the world some peace.

JIMMY. Now John, we can't let those people turn us around just by beating on our bodies. That's what I found out. It isn't about them.

JOHN. It looks like you and me we've changed places, haven't we?

JIMMY. No, we haven't changed places we've come together. I did it because I love you John.

JOHN. I love you too Jimmy.

ELLEN. Hold on Jimmy. We'll get there just hold on. …Jimmy? Jimmy. Jimmy!

Jimmy exits the car and stands in a spotlight.

JIMMY. I feel like in a dream where I am flying. Circling like a hawk rising up in a warm column of clean, sweet air. All the pain and the fear and hatred have left me and I suddenly realize that I am not alone but now among the many.

A song like "Freedom Is a Constant Struggle" plays.

Scene 8

The Democratic National Convention, Atlantic City, New Jersey. July 22nd, 1964. Lights up. Ellen is waiting…

Enter John.

ELLEN. John where have you been? We're late. Mrs. Fannie Lou Hamer is about to speak. Come on or we'll miss it.

JOHN. No Ellen, I'm not going.

ELLEN. You're not going? What do you mean you're not going?

JOHN. I'm not going to hear Mrs. Fannie Lou Hamer speak or to anything else in this fucking convention.

ELLEN. John, what is it? What happened?

35

JOHN. First of all no one is going to hear Mrs. Fannie Lou Hamer speak. Not on television anyway. Not across the country as we had hoped. No, President Johnson is suddenly having a television news broadcast to address the nation in just a few moments when Fanny Lou Hamer is about to speak. The world will be watching him and not her. She's being "blacked out" so to speak.

ELLEN. Oh, my God.

JOHN. Johnson signed the Civil Rights bill, but he still wants the Dixiecrats to vote for him come November. He's a vote counter and he's not going to let all those delegate votes just go away. The Black folks in the Mississippi Freedom Democratic Party don't have a chance of being seated in this convention. It's all rigged.

ELLEN. Rigged? Rigged? But, how can it be rigged? This is a democracy.

JOHN. A democracy for you and me maybe…

ELLEN. I can't accept that… Those Black folks in Mississippi they did all the right things. They did everything they were supposed to do to be citizens. Whether it was losing their jobs, or being locked in jail or thrown off their land, hunger, privation, their children harassed and their love ones murdered…like the three civil rights workers, like Jimmy… And now that they've made it here you're saying that their votes don't count?

JOHN. No, they don't.

ELLEN. I can't accept that.

JOHN. Johnson's running mate, Hubert Humphrey, has come here to Atlantic City to make a deal. The Mississippi Freedom Democratic Party gets two…I said just two seats at large with no voting privileges at this convention, while the regular, white Mississippi Democratic Party gets to do what they've always done and that's run Mississippi politics the way they see fit. That's your democracy.

ELLEN. The Mississippi Freedom Democratic Party is not going to agree to that.

JOHN. If they don't then there's nothing. No place at the table, none.

ELLEN. Then what are we going to do John?

JOHN. There's nothing we can do. It's over, finished.

ELLEN. But how can it be finished. We didn't do what we set out to do. It can't be finished.

JOHN. Yes Ellen, it's finished, over, done with. Besides they don't want us anymore. That's all the SNCC workers are talking about now, and even the leadership, is "Black Power, Black Power," self-determination and racial independence.

ELLEN. And why shouldn't they see it that way? They've been isolated...betrayed.

JOHN. Yes, but Ellen, you and me we are not betraying them.

ELLEN. Oh no? And how would they know that? We're white John and every white person they've ever known has suppressed their lives. So how are they going to know just by looking at us what is the difference between us and everything else they should fear in their lives? How? How do they know that? Tell me, how?

JOHN. Ellen I know how you feel. I feel the same way too. But it's hopeless. We just have to move on, that's all.

ELLEN. Move on? Move on to what? Move on to where?

JOHN. Well, I've been thinking about going on to New York or maybe Chicago and joining up with the one of the organizations that's resisting the war.

ELLEN. ...War? What war John?

JOHN. ...The Vietnam War.

ELLEN. ...The Vietnam War? John there's a war right here. It's a war for freedom and justice and equality. How can you protest for a war over there when there's a war right here fighting over the same things?

JOHN. Yes Ellen, you're right, it is the same fight. ...And why not? There isn't anything more we can do here. They don't want us anymore Ellen.

ELLEN. Then they'll have to tell me that to my face.

JOHN. Come on Ellen, come with me.

ELLEN. Come with you? Come with you where?

JOHN. To Chicago or New York, they've got a strong war resistance movement in Brooklyn.

ELLEN. You're going to quit aren't you? You're going to quit and you want to take me with you. You want me to quit too.

JOHN. No, I'm not giving up the fight. I'm just changing course that's all. But I'm leaving SNCC. SNCC is breaking up. It's splitting up over race. They don't want us Ellen. They say that it isn't our fight. And maybe they're right, but I can't bear to see it go down. So, I'm just taking the fight to another place.

ELLEN. And what place is that John?

JOHN. It's important work Ellen. It's a fight where we could make a difference. What do you say?

ELLEN. No! I don't want to be around a bunch of white boys arguing about something that happened in Russia in the 1930s. There's a resistance here and it's happening now. I mean why do you want me to go with you anyhow?

JOHN. You don't know?

ELLEN. Know what?

JOHN. Ellen...I...I want us to be together.

ELLEN. Oh John...John. I'm sorry John. I don't know what to say.

JOHN. Don't say anything. Just try it. Just let's get away and start over again.

ELLEN. I can't do that John.

JOHN. Why not?

ELLEN. It surprises me that you don't know the answer to that. I thought you cared.

JOHN. But I do care Ellen, I do.

ELLEN. No you don't. You don't even understand. You see I've thought a lot about the things that you're thinking about now. About how I have a choice, how I can get away and move on...start all over again and give myself another chance. People like us take that for granted like it was an entitlement from God. But what it really is John, it's a privilege. One that we should thank God we're blessed enough to have. And me, I never knew what a privilege it really was 'til I went down to Mississippi. I can't turn back now. I'm giving up my turn to choose.

JOHN. But I love you Ellen.

ELLEN. I'm sorry John. I didn't know. I had no idea. But I can't go away with you just because *you* feel that way.

JOHN. It's because of Jimmy isn't it?

ELLEN. Because of Jimmy what?

JOHN. You couldn't see me for seeing Jimmy.

ELLEN. You never said anything John. All you ever talk about is... ideas. Something that's happened in the past or it's something that hasn't really happened yet. Jimmy...he was an idea. He still is.

JOHN. It was after Jimmy's death really, that I realized that I couldn't do this anymore. ...I felt responsible.

ELLEN. You felt responsible for Jimmy's death?

JOHN. Yes.

ELLEN. We're all responsible for Jimmy's death. Mississippi, this country, the world, even Jimmy himself, we're all responsible.

JOHN. Yeah, and no matter how much suffering you see, somehow it never really gets beyond the abstract until it happens to someone you know. And then it gets...

ELLEN. ...Personal?

JOHN. Yes, it gets personal. That was the thing about Jimmy. He was always in your face, up front and personal. And he was always willing to make the ultimate sacrifice. I can see that now. And when he finally makes the ultimate sacrifice he makes it for me.

ELLEN. Jimmy didn't make that sacrifice just for you John he made it for all of us. He made it for himself. Look John we can't all be like Jimmy. All we can do is to do the best we can.

JOHN. Where did you get all wise all of a sudden?

ELLEN. I got wise down in Mississippi with Jimmy and you.

JOHN. I have to confess that I was powerfully jealous of the two of you. I struggled with that Ellen. I still do. You see, I liked you...I mean I had feelings for you from the first moment I saw you in that hallway at Western College back in Ohio. You were just so full of amazement and wonder. I loved that. Geez...I don't know. But there was Jimmy. There was always Jimmy. I couldn't get past Jimmy. It's like he's standing here right now. I couldn't find the words to let you know that I love you Ellen.

ELLEN. ...You don't love me because of me and Jimmy, do you John?

JOHN. No…I don't think so.

ELLEN. I really hope that's true.

JOHN. …Me too.

ELLEN. Look John I'm going to go. I don't want to miss, Mrs. Fannie Lou Hamer. Maybe the world won't be watching her but I will. …Good luck John.

JOHN. And good luck to you Ellen.

Ellen exits. John alone…

Scene 9

VOICE OF THE INTERVIEWER. We are listening now to the voice of Mrs. Fannie Lou Hamer, the chairwoman of the Black Mississippi Freedom Democratic Party.

FANNIE LOU HAMER. Mr. Chairman, and the Credentials Committee of the Democratic National Convention of 1964, my name is Mrs. Fannie Lou Hamer, and I live at 626 East Lafayette Street, Ruleville, Mississippi, Sunflower County, the home of Senator James O. Eastland, and Senator Stennis. On the 31st of August of 1962, eighteen of us traveled twenty-six miles to the county court-house in Indianola, Mississippi, to try to register to vote and to become first-class citizens. But we were met by the Highway Patrol and only two of us were allowed to take the literacy test. Meanwhile our bus driver was arrested and charged with driving a bus that was the wrong color. We paid our fine and then I discover when I get back home that the plantation owner who owns the land we lived on and sharecropped for over eighteen years says that we got to go because we tried to register to vote. On September 10th, 1962, sixteen bullets were fired into the home of Mr. and Mrs. Robert Tucker where my family and me, we had been staying. And on that same night two young girls were shot in Ruleville. They say their parents were involved in registering. Another time on June 9th, 1963, we were coming back from a voter registration workshop and when we got off the bus in Montgomery County we were arrested. They called us horrible names. One young girl they beat her so long that she cried then she hollered and then she prayed. And terrible as it was I was so glad to hear her prayers because they come and beat me too. They made two convict colored boys beat me with blackjacks until they were tired. All of this is on account of us wanting to register to become first-class citizens. And if the Mississippi Freedom Democratic Party, which represents all of Mississippi citizens, represents the majority of Mississippi citizens and not just white Mississippians, if we are not seated now, then I question America. Is this the America, the land of the free and the home of the brave where we have to sleep with our telephones off the hook because we fear for our lives and being threatened daily because we want to live as decent human beings in America? Is this the America that has been promised to all of us? I ask you! Where is America?

Scene 10

An interview. Ellen stands in a spotlight.

VOICE OF THE INTERVIEWER. Crowds are just now coming out of the convention hall where Mrs. Fanny Lou Hamer has just addressed the convention delegates here in Atlantic City, New Jersey. We have here with us Miss Ellen Bormann, Vassar class of '67, who was one of close to a thousand volunteers from largely prestigious Ivy League schools around the country who went down to Mississippi this summer to register Mississippi Negroes to vote. Miss Bormann why did you decide to take on such a task?

ELLEN. Because if we the white students didn't go down to Mississippi to work with the people and live with the people of Mississippi then no one in the country would have taken any notice. Their struggle has been going on for a long time and no one noticed before now.

VOICE OF THE INTERVIEWER. And what was it like living with Mississippi Negroes?

ELLEN. I found them to be the kindest, friendly and most generous people of any group of people I've ever met. It was wonderful really.

VOICE OF THE INTERVIEWER. That's very interesting. And what

41

happens now that both the Black Mississippi Freedom Democratic Party and the regular White Mississippi Democratic Party have left the convention in protest?

ELLEN. We will just have to regroup and redouble our efforts. The issues are too important to stop now. We've got to keep up the struggle.

VOICE OF THE INTERVIEWER. Yes, but surely now that the convention is over as far as you are concerned, and the summer is over you must have thoughts about going back home. You're heading into your junior year. Will you head back to Vassar? After all this, what are you going to do with the rest of your life Miss Ellen Bormann?

ELLEN. I don't know what I'm going to do with the rest of my life, but whatever I do there is one thing I know for sure... That whenever I encounter oppression and injustice I'm going to say something about it... I'm going to speak out... I'm going to try to stop it... I'm going to fight... I'm going to resist.

Music plays, a song like "Ain't Gonna Let Nobody Turn Me Around."

End of Play

PROPERTY LIST
(Use this space to create props lists for your production)

SOUND EFFECTS
(Use this space to create sound effects lists for your production)

Note on Songs/Recordings, Images, or Other Production Design Elements

Be advised that Dramatists Play Service, Inc., neither holds the rights to nor grants permission to use any songs, recordings, images, or other design elements mentioned in the play. It is the responsibility of the producing theater/organization to obtain permission of the copyright owner(s) for any such use. Additional royalty fees may apply for the right to use copyrighted materials.

For any songs/recordings, images, or other design elements mentioned in the play, works in the public domain may be substituted. It is the producing theater/organization's responsibility to ensure the substituted work is indeed in the public domain. Dramatists Play Service, Inc., cannot advise as to whether or not a song/arrangement/recording, image, or other design element is in the public domain.